This is Christmas

Daily Inspirations for the Advent Season

David Vogel

With a foreword by Kathy Troccoli

This is Christmas: Daily Reflections for the Advent Season

© 2022 David Vogel

All rights reserved. No portion of this book may be reproduced, stored in a retrieval system, or transmitted in any form or by any means—electronic, mechanical, photocopy, recording, scanning, or other—except for brief quotations in critical reviews or articles, without the prior written permission of the publisher.

Published by Vogel Design LLC
Learn more about the author at davidbvogel.com and on Instagram @yep.its.dave

Vogel, David
    This is Christmas / David Vogel
    Vogel Design LLC
    ISBN 9798840153352

Scripture quotations marked (ESV) are from The ESV® Bible (The Holy Bible, English Standard Version®), copyright © 2001 by Crossway, a publishing ministry of Good News Publishers. Used by permission. All rights reserved. Scriptures marked (KJV) are taken from the King James Version, public domain in the United States. Rights in the Authorized (King James) Version in the United Kingdom are vested in the Crown. Published by permission of the Crown's patentee, Cambridge University. Scripture quotations marked (NASB) are taken from the New American Standard Bible® (NASB). Copyright © 1960, 1962, 1963, 1968, 1971, 1972, 1973, 1975, 1977, 1995, 2020 by The Lockman Foundation. Used by permission. www.Lockman.org. Scripture quotations marked (NIV) are taken from the Holy Bible, New International Version®, NIV®. Copyright © 1973, 1978, 1984, 2011 by Biblica, Inc.® Used by permission of Zondervan. All rights reserved worldwide. www.zondervan.com. The "NIV" and "New International Version" are trademarks registered in the United States Patent and Trademark Office by Biblica, Inc.® Scripture quotations marked (NKJV) are taken from the New King James Version®. Copyright © 1982 by Thomas Nelson. Used by permission. All rights reserved. Scripture quotations marked (NLT) are taken from the Holy Bible, New Living Translation, copyright © 1996, 2004, 2015 by Tyndale House Foundation. Used by permission of Tyndale House Publishers, Carol Stream, Illinois 60188. All rights reserved. Scripture quotations marked (NLV) are taken from the New Life Version, Copyright © 1969 and 2003. Used by permission of Barbour Publishing, Inc., Uhrichsville, Ohio 44683. All rights reserved. Scripture quotations marked (MSG) are taken from The Message, copyright © 1993, 2002, 2018 by Eugene H. Peterson. Used by permission of NavPress. All rights reserved. Represented by Tyndale House Publishers. Scripture quotations marked (TPT) are from The Passion Translation®. Copyright © 2017, 2018, 2020 by Passion & Fire Ministries, Inc. Used by permission. All rights reserved. ThePassionTranslation.com.

Song lyrics, book and film quotations, and other cited references are used by the author for illustration purposes only and are the sole intellectual and/or commercial property of the respective copyright owners.

Cover artwork, graphic design, and typesetting by Vogel Design LLC in Wichita, Kansas.

Author photo by Asher Isaac.

Adobe Stock images on the cover and throughout are used under Adobe's Standard License (stock.adobe.com/license-terms). All other images are generously provided by photographers on unsplash.com.

For my daughters
Claire & Chloe
Never lose your wonder of His love

And in memory of
Grandma Helen
& Grandpa Ray
*who taught me how to honor Christmas well
and keep it in my heart all the year*

Foreword by Kathy Troccoli

I met David years ago, when I asked him to become a graphic designer and website creator for me. I was not only taken with His expertise in this area, but more taken with his kindness and earnestness to do things with excellence. I soon discovered his quick wit and humor. It made working with him such a delight. Then much to my surprise, I heard him sing. A beautiful tone of expression came out of this man that touched my soul, and I knew blessed the heart of the One he was singing about.

When David asked me to write this foreword, why would I not be surprised that he would be an author, too? He is a multifaceted, gifted man.

Christmas has always been my favorite time of year, but as is the case for so many of us, it's so easy to let the Christmas season pass us by without its eternal significance coming alive in our hearts. My friend David's writings in this book will bring you back to the true meaning of what Christmas is all about.

Jesus used storytelling masterfully

·····>

in His parables to convey supernatural truths. This powerful yet simple means of communication brought understanding to the limitation of our own thoughts and views of life. This way of speaking opened the eyes of those who truly listened. Revelation came. How fitting that David would communicate in a similar way, and that Christmas could be a time when people experience its life-changing significance.

The decorating, the parties, the gift buying and giving... there is a busyness around the holiday season that lends to forgetting the whole reason for celebration. Our hearts need to be turned back to the simple yet stunning truth that our Savior was born. With that came redemption, new life, joy, hope, and a love that would never leave us.

As you turn the pages of *This is Christmas*, you can't help but turn your focus to the Messiah that was born into this broken world to heal our broken hearts.

Whether you wake up in the morning and read each devotional to start your day, sit down with your family and read them out loud, or send one to a friend who needs encouragement—this offering of David's is sure to be a treasure for years to come.

Kathy Troccoli
Singer, songwriter & author

✣ Introduction

Welcome to Advent, the beginning of—as Andy Williams proclaimed—the most wonderful time of the year. This season is a busy dash through the snow toward Christmas Day. We've got shopping and wrapping and programs and parties... The list goes on. I'm the son of a children's pastor (Mom) and church musician (Dad), and now a pastor and church musician myself, I can attest fully to the hecticness of the season.

I felt called to write this collection of devotionals so that you and I might pause that chaos. My hope is that each day, at least briefly, we can take our eyes off the to-do list and focus on what Christmas really is: remembering and celebrating the birth of Jesus Christ, the Hope of the World.

In the liturgical Church calendar, Advent marks the season leading to Christmas. Often simplified as the first 25 days of December, the actual Advent calendar starts the fourth Sunday before Christmas Day. Depending on the year, Advent can be as short as 21 days or as long as 28 (plus Christmas Day itself).

To accommodate any year, this book includes 29 devotionals: one for each day starting on November 27 through December 25.

My prayer is that you will be encouraged, refreshed, and challenged by the Truths that we find in the nativity story, throughout the Scriptures, and reflected around us in our daily lives. The gifts, lights, decorations, music, movies, and ugly (beautiful!) sweaters we enjoy are a joyous part of the celebration. But the *reason* we celebrate is Jesus. This is the wonder of God's love. This the hope of Jesus our Savior. And this is the joy we have in eternal life with Him.

This is Christmas!

NOV 27

The Thrill of Hope

I enjoy looking at the presents under the Christmas tree much more than I do unwrapping them. I know, that's weird. But I love the excitement of imagining what might be inside the glittery paper. The experience of anticipation brings me so much joy!

I'm the same way with trips. Even as I'm writing this first draft, my wife, Hanna, and I have a short Caribbean cruise planned for the fall. I periodically log into our cruise account, and it shows me the number of days until we weigh anchor. I just checked: 97 to go. Ninety-seven days to prepare, to daydream, and to be filled with excitement for what's to come.

This is the thrill of hope. It's the certainty of something to come. It's the proof of things that will be, but are not yet seen (Hebrews 11:1). And that's where we begin this Advent journey.

The prophets promised that a Messiah, a Savior, was coming to rescue Israel. Hooray! And yet...

Isaiah prophesied about Jesus 700 years before He would be born. In those last 400, there was complete prophetic silence. Long lay the world in sin and error pining, the hymn says.

Long lay the world.

Can you imagine that kind of wait? How easy it is for us to get disillusioned when what we've been promised does not come immediately. Our expectation grows cold; anticipation fades to cynicism. King Solomon wrote that hope deferred makes the heart sick (Proverbs 13:12). The poet Langston Hughes wrote that a dream deferred "dries up like a raisin in the sun," or "just sags like a heavy load" (*Harlem*, 1951).

When we lose confidence in a promise—when we lose the thrill of hope—excited expectation turns to a heavy, lifeless burden. But the promises of God are not empty! In Hebrews 10:23, Paul writes, "Let us hold unswervingly to the hope we profess, for he who promised is faithful" (NIV).

God is faithful. Jesus is faithful.

In these next few weeks leading to Christmas, the day we celebrate Jesus's birth, join me in experiencing the anticipation of each day. Don't get bogged down in the busyness and chaos of the season, thinking, *I'll celebrate on Christmas Day.* No, immerse yourself now in the expectant anticipation of what's to come and let your weary soul rejoice!

Experience the thrill of hope.

> Christmas is when you get stuff!
> You need more toys!
>
> **BUZZ-SAW LOUIE IN**
> *VEGGIETALES: THE TOY THAT SAVED CHRISTMAS*

NOV 28

The Gift of God's Presence

The irony is not lost on anyone that the day after Thanksgiving—which we've set aside to express gratitude for all that we have—is a day dedicated to shopping. And shopping. And more shopping.

Black Friday officially kicks off the holiday shopping season, but I'd like to suggest that Thanksgiving should kick off the Christmas season. Thanksgiving is 100% a part of the Christmas season.

The wait-your-turn-Santa crowd might disagree, but I stand by that statement—and not just because it lets me put my tree up earlier. Gratitude should permeate every aspect of our Christmas celebrations. A wonderful reminder of this is in Josh Groban's 2007 Christmas album, *Noël*, which includes a song called "Thankful":

Some days we forget to look around us.
Some days we can't see the joy that surrounds us.
So caught up inside ourselves, we take when we should give....
There's so much to be thankful for.

····>

The stuff of this world is a distraction. And I admit, I am a consummate consumer. For better or worse, my favorite part of any museum or theme park is the gift shop that they make you walk through to exit. In a way, we've set Christmas up to be the month-long gift shop we have to walk through to exit the year. No one gets out without a souvenir!

But Christmas should not point us to the presents. Christmas should point us to God's *presence*—Jesus, Emmanuel, God With Us. And (at the risk of using too many puns in one paragraph) while Black Friday puts our focus on the savings, Christmas should put our focus on the *Savior*.

When we lose sight of our gratitude to God, we forget that He—our Father of Heavenly Lights—is the giver of every good and perfect gift (James 1:17). He will give everything we need: salvation through Jesus.

One of the names given to God in the Old Testament is Jehovah-Jireh. It means God (Jehovah) Will Provide (Jireh).

"Jehovah-Jireh" is translated from the Hebrew *YHWH-Yireh*. Scholars have pointed out that the letters "YHWH" (to which we later added vowels to create the word "Yahweh") are representative of breathing sounds. Inhale, *yh*, exhale, *wh*.

The very air in our lungs is a proclamation of God's good gifts. Each breath that enters our lips is a confirmation of God's provision, and each exhale should be a praise of thanksgiving: "Let us give thanks all the time to God through Jesus Christ. Our gift to Him is to give thanks. Our lips should always give thanks to His name" (Hebrews 13:15 NLV).

Jesus is the gift God gave us for Christmas, and our every breath of gratitude is a gift back to Him. There's so much to be thankful for!

*A thrill of hope, the weary world rejoices.
For yonder breaks a new and glorious morn'.*
"O HOLY NIGHT" BY JOHN SULLIVAN DWIGHT

NOV 29

The Good Earth

"In the beginning God created the heavens and the earth."

Those 10 words begin the story of creation. In Genesis 1 we read of the six days God worked by speaking our world into existence.

"God called the dry land Earth, and He saw that it was good."

But by 1968, things didn't seem so good. In America, that bloody, catastrophic year saw the assassinations of Martin Luther King, Jr., and Robert Kennedy, racial injustice, anger and fear about wars overseas, and bloody riots and protests back home. By the time NASA launched its Apollo 8 mission on December 21, the world was weary.

After the three-day trip to the moon, astronauts Frank Borman, Jim Lovelle, and Bill Anders became the first humans to orbit another world. It was Christmas Eve.

With millions watching back on Earth, NASA began a live broadcast

····>

....> as the Apollo 8 Command Module approached lunar sunrise. "We were told that...we would have the largest audience that had ever listened to a human voice," Borman later recalled. "And the only instructions that we got from NASA was to do something appropriate."

As they beamed home live images of the moon and Earth, the three astronauts took turns reading Genesis 1:1-10.

In the beginning God created the heavens and the earth...

They signed off with this: "From the crew of Apollo 8, we close with good night, good luck, a Merry Christmas, and God bless all of you, all of you on the good Earth." At the end of a tumultuous year, from their view out in the heavens, these three space pioneers looked out upon the earth and pronounced it good.

God sent Jesus into the world to save it, not condemn it (John 3:17). There was, however, plenty to condemn. Violence, injustice, greed, ungodliness... The world was a mess then as it is now. In every story we read from the Old Testament, we see the world sick in sin and error, pining for a Savior.

And just as He had at the very beginning of creation, God looked down at the world. He saw Jesus preparing to begin His ministry. And He said, "This is my Son, whom I love; with him I am well pleased" (Matthew 3:17 NIV).

God looked down and saw Jesus, ready to begin the work of redeeming His beloved creation. And He pronounced Jesus good.

Photo courtesy of NASA.

This is *Earthrise,* taken on Christmas Eve 1968 by astronaut Bill Anders as the Apollo 8 spacecraft circumnavigated the moon. This was the first time humans ever witnessed the earth rising over the horizon of the lunar surface below. More than 50 years later, this image still inspires wonder and awe... It's one of my favorite photographs, and I couldn't help including it in this book!

For God, who said, "Let light shine out of darkness," made his light shine in our hearts to give us the light of the knowledge of God's glory displayed in the face of Christ.

2 CORINTHIANS 4:6 NIV

NOV 30

✺ Christmas Lights

Friday nights in December are often spent the same way for our family: in the car, hot cocoa in hand, driving through the local neighborhoods that are known for their dazzling Christmas light displays. We have Edward Hibberd Johnson to thank for this.

Part engineer, part businessman, and part circus ringmaster, Johnson is credited for making many of Thomas Edison's inventions commercially successful. A *Smithsonian Magazine* article reports that in 1882, after Edison patented the light bulb, one went off over Johnson's head.

He hand-wired 80 bulbs together and strung them around a Christmas tree mounted on a spinning base. Then he called the press. "At the rear of the beautiful parlors, was a large Christmas tree presenting a most picturesque and uncanny aspect," Detroit reporter W.A. Croffut wrote. "It was brilliantly lighted…. One can hardly imagine anything prettier."

Gone were the days of candles dangerously pinned to brittle pine branches. Christmas lights were here to stay!

It's fitting that lights are such an important part of our Christmas celebrations. Isaiah prophesied that "the people who walk in darkness will see a great light. For those who live in a land of deep darkness, a light will shine" (Isaiah 9:2 NLT).

That light was Jesus. He said, "I am the light of the world. Whoever

·····>

follows me will not walk in darkness, but will have the light of life" (John 8:12 ESV).

The thing about light is, it really doesn't take much to break the darkness.

Theatre houses use something called a "ghost light," which is an exposed bulb atop a tall stand that lights the stage between performances. A safety practice steeped in tradition (and superstition), this single, small light illuminates the dark, empty auditorium.

The light shines in the darkness, and the darkness has not overcome it (John 1:5 NIV).

As believers, we are called into the marvelous light of Jesus (1 Peter 2:9). And when we step into that light, we become God's children of light ourselves (Ephesians 5:8). In a traditional Christmas Eve candlelight service, a single candle is used to slowly ignite the candles held by every person in the church. In the same way, we are called to spread the light of Jesus to everyone we meet.

The God who spoke light into the vastness of a dark universe spoke light into your heart. Now, Jesus says *we* are to be the light of the world: "Let your light shine before others, that they may see your good deeds and glorify your Father in heaven" (Matthew 5:16 NIV).

Be the light to someone this Christmas. It may be the only light they have, and it will brighten their life more than you know.

"I've come at last," said he. "She has kept me out for a long time, but I have got in at last. Aslan is on the move. The Witch's magic is weakening."

FATHER CHRISTMAS
IN *THE LION, THE WITCH, AND THE WARDROBE*
BY C. S. LEWIS

DEC 1

Always Winter and Never Christmas

"It is winter in Narnia, and has been for ever so long," Mr. Tumnus said. "Always winter and never Christmas."

I remember hearing those words for the first time as a child. Dad read C. S. Lewis's *The Chronicles of Narnia* series to my brother and me more than once. Even then, just a few years old and hearing these words from *The Lion, the Witch, and the Wardrobe*, I felt their weight.

Young Lucy had just arrived in a snowy forest of Narnia through—what else?—an enchanted closet. The soft fur coats that brushed her face turned to prickly fir trees, and she found herself at a lamppost, talking to a faun named Tumnus. The White Witch put a curse over Narnia, he told Lucy, casting it into eternal winter.

Always winter and never Christmas.

Sometimes there seems to be no hope. We face the burdens of finances, stress at work, a struggling marriage, estranged children, caring for aging parents, exhaustion, isolation, anxiety, grief, depression... Or we look into the world and see natural catastrophes, social unrest, persecution, prejudice, injustice,

·····>

wars, violence, and mass shootings.

So much fear. So much hurt. So much death. So much despair.

It can feel like an endless winter—clouded, colorless, and coated in ice. But the White Witch does not have the final say.

As the book continues, Lucy and her siblings learn of a lion named Aslan. He's wild, not tame. He isn't safe, but he's good. He's the King, and he's out to end the winter.

The prophet writes in Isaiah 43:19 that God is doing a new thing. He's on the move.

Aslan is such a wonderful portrait of Jesus. Jesus cannot be tamed to the expectations of this world because He answers only to the commission of Heaven. He isn't safe because He works with reckless abandon to seek out every single person wherever they are, regardless of their failures or sin.

He's good because He brings all of Heaven to Earth. And He's the King because He is the Son of God and one with God, the Creator and Ruler of the universe.

We don't need to worry; He's got this. "Look at the birds of the air; they do not sow or reap or store away in barns, and yet your heavenly Father feeds them," Jesus says in Luke 6:26-27 (NIV). "Are you not much more valuable than they? Can any one of you by worrying add a single hour to your life?"

Jesus came from on high to draw us near to Him, to give us hope for the future. He will disperse the clouds of gloom and night, and He will banish death's dark shadow. Rejoice! Rejoice! Emmanuel—Jesus—is here!

Sometimes this world feels like an endless winter in Narnia. But Aslan is on the move, and Christmas is coming.

Stargazing

The year 2020 was pretty rotten. The COVID-19 pandemic shut down the entire world. Commerce, travel, and relationships ground to a halt as we sheltered in place or practiced social distancing.

For months, our fragmented society staggered on with minimal interaction. We tried to work from home via Zoom conferences. Sharing life with loved ones was done over FaceTime or social media. And church congregations tuned

DEC 2

When you wish upon a star,
Makes no difference who you are,
Anything your heart desires
Will come to you.

JIMINY CRICKET IN WALT DISNEY'S
PINOCCHIO

in for pre-recorded or live-streamed worship services. It was depressing and lonely.

But on December 21, 2020, something unusual happened—something that hadn't happened for nearly 800 years. Jupiter and Saturn aligned so closely that, from our vantage point, they seemed to almost collide in the night sky. Nearly overlapping, the two planets created a radiant point of light in the inky dark. Happening just days before Christmas, many called it "The Bethlehem Star."

Our family drove into the country for a better view. We were not alone. I was surprised

····>

by the dozens of idling cars that lined the dirt roads, every single person gazing upward. At the end of a year that did nothing but isolate, this moment drew millions together in the simple, synchronized action of looking up at a dazzling new star.

Two thousand years earlier, another dazzling new star shown in the heavens. The *real* Bethlehem Star. A group of stargazers saw it appear, and they recognized its significance.

"Where is the newborn king of the Jews?" they asked. "We saw his star as it rose, and we have come to worship him" (Matthew 2:2 NLT).

These Magi from the east knew where to look. They recognized a King had come. They understood a brand-new Kingdom was rising—a Kingdom meant to bring all people together by reuniting them with God their Creator through their Savior Jesus Christ.

Jesus's birth, marked by this sparkling new star, began a new age for humankind. What we call the "end times" is simply the countdown to when Jesus will return. In Luke 21, Jesus is telling His disciples how they will know they are living in these times: "When all these things begin to happen," Jesus said, "stand and *look up*, for your salvation is near" (verse 28 NLT, my emphasis).

When each of us is looking in the same direction—at Jesus—we have unity with one-another. When each of us is looking up—at Heaven—we see our salvation. Only when we are looking up together will we see and remember our collective hope in Jesus Christ.

The Bethlehem Star still shines in your heart. Keep looking up.

So then, prepare your hearts and minds for action! Stay alert and fix your hope firmly on the marvelous grace that is coming to you. For when Jesus Christ is unveiled, a greater measure of grace will be released to you.

1 PETER 1:13 TPT

Prepare the Way

A couple of years ago, we decided to purchase our very first robot vacuum cleaner. With two toddlers, our floors were frequently covered by Cheerios, goldfish-shaped crackers, and rainbow sundae sprinkles (don't ask). The thought of an automated vacuum that could tidy up for us was appealing.

Our oldest, then four, named her Rose.

Rose is very good at what she does. (And considering all the Cheerios she's consumed, her good cholesterol has to be through the roof!) With the tap of a button, she comes to life and makes a clean sweep of whatever rooms we've asked her to work on before returning to her dock and going back to sleep.

However, if there are toys scattered on the floor, or if some pieces of furniture are out of place, Rose can't do her job. She'll clumsily bump into things, miss spots, or high-center and become stranded. So, before we activate Rose, we have to pick things up around the house to clear a path and prepare the way for her.

As I was doing that the other day, I was reminded of Isaiah's prophecy about John the Baptist, who would come before Jesus to announce His arrival:

"The voice of one crying in the wilderness: 'Prepare the way of the Lord; make straight in the desert a highway for our God. Every valley

·····>

shall be exalted, and every mountain and hill brought low; the crooked places shall be made straight and the rough places smooth'" (Isaiah 40:3-4 NKJV).

John is telling Israel that their long-awaited Messiah is coming. So clear the way! Give Him a direct path! The glory of the Lord is about to be revealed, John was saying, and you don't want to miss out.

The Bethlehem innkeeper certainly did. He failed to make room for Mary and Joseph (Luke 2:7). As a result, he missed the opportunity to welcome Jesus into this world. He missed the blessing of the very first Christmas.

Is your mind cluttered? Is your heart crowded? Have you found that when you do have some open space, there's always something ready to fill it?

To leave room for Jesus—to prepare the way for Him—takes intentionality and effort and practice. Like I have to do before I can let Rose vacuum, we need to sift through our lives and find the things that might crowd Jesus out; the things that are getting in the way of what He wants to do in you, for you, and through you.

"Let every heart prepare Him room." We sing these words this time each year. But this Christmas, let's apply them directly to our lives. Let's prepare the way for our Savior!

Every Day is Christmas

My wife, Hanna, has a recurring calendar event set in her phone for every December 26. Its title: "David gets sad."

Early in our marriage, she learned that I sink into a brief depression when all the festivities of Christmas are over. This reminds her to give me a little extra space, grace, and affection as the lights come down and the ornaments go back into storage.

I love Christmas. I love the music and gifts. I love the anticipation and the celebration. I love the eggnog and sugar cookies and apple cider. So when it's over, I get sad.

And I get sad because I fail to remember this important truth: Christmas is every day.

Before Jesus's sacrifice, sin separated us from God. A blood offering merely covered over a person's transgression, and it expired as soon as he or she sinned again.

Do not pass Go, and do not collect $200.

But then Jesus came: fully God and fully human, humbly born as a helpless baby. He came to die on the cross as our final sacrifice. His blood did not merely cover over

·····>

our sins, but it wiped them clean forever.

Jesus's birth reset the clock for humanity: the hourglass was flipped, and the sands of time that had been marking down the days to His arrival began amassing the days that we are redeemed to God.

Second Corinthians 1:10 says that Jesus saved us once, and He'll stick with us forever: "We have placed our confidence in him, and he will continue to rescue us" (NLT).

And so every day is Christmas. If Jesus resides in your heart, your body and your spirit should be a living celebration. Your words are the twinkle lights that show others the Truth. Your actions are the frosted sugar cookies that sweeten the lives of others. Your compassion is the softly-falling snow that brings peace to the hurting. Your generosity is the beautifully-wrapped gift for others to find under the tree.

We don't need the lights or cookies or snow or gifts to make Christmas *Christmas*, because Christmas is in us. The calendar sets December 25 aside to commemorate Jesus's birth. But that birthday has far too many eternal implications to assign it just a season, let alone a single day. We have hope in Jesus's return and faith in His promises that should cause us to celebrate all year long.

I love how Charles Dickens ends *A Christmas Carol*. As he speaks of Ebenezer Scrooge, he also speaks to the way we should live: "It was always said of him that he knew how to keep Christmas well, if any man alive possessed the knowledge. May that be truly said of us, and all of us!"

Mortals, join the mighty chorus which the morning stars began.
"THE HYMN OF JOY" BY HENRY VAN DYKE

Heaven and Nature Sing

DEC 5

Worship and celebration through music is my favorite part of the Christmas season, and almost every Christmas carol holds a unique memory.

"Hark! The Harold Angels Sing" from Mannheim Steamroller's *A Fresh Aire Christmas* album takes me back to helping my dad fluff branches on our artificial tree. Josh Groban's arrangement of "Silent Night" from his *Noël* album holds memories of late-night/early-morning car rides to Black Friday shopping. My grandparents had an antique set of decorative electric bells that would ring out "Here We Come A-Caroling." And "O Little Town of Bethlehem" will forever be linked in my memory to a string of singing Christmas lights my parents had when I was a child; I can still hear the digital tone of early-90s technology playing that tune from the small speaker box on the end of the cord. (Not to mention... Anything on Michael Bublé's 2011 *Christmas* album sparks instant yuletide bliss.)

We love our Christmas carols. But I don't think praising through music is exclusive to just humans, and this lyric in "Joy to the World" has always stuck out to me for that reason: "Let every heart prepare Him room, and Heaven and nature sing."

Heaven and nature are singing!

God loves songs of praise so much that he orchestrated it into the very foundation of His creation.

·····>

·····>

Pause now and read Psalm 148. It winds its way through all of nature, commanding praise from the sun, moon, stars, lightning, hail, stormy winds, snow, clouds, mountains, hills, ocean depths, trees, wild animals, sea creatures, small creatures, cattle, and birds. "Let them praise the name of the Lord, for at his command they were created" (Psalm 148:5 NIV).

It's not until the end of this list that humans are finally instructed to worship. Nature was praising God long before we ever got started.

Not only that, but praise is such an intrinsic part of God's creation that it groans under the weight of this expectation. When the Pharisees criticized the celebration of Jesus's arrival at Jerusalem, He responded (Luke 19:40 TPT), "If my followers were silenced, the very stones would break forth with praises!"

Nature is eagerly waiting to declare the reign of Jesus Christ, our Lord. Creation is a living hymn! The moment believers cease our worship, creation will burst into song in our place.

This Christmas, don't let your voice go silent. Join with the carols that were written at the dawn of creation. Join with the good tidings that were first sung by angels to shepherds. Join with the hymns of celebration and praise that are ringing around you today!

> Everyone was gripped with great wonder and awe, and they praised God, exclaiming, "We have seen amazing things today!"
>
> LUKE 5:26 NLT

DEC 6

Lost in the Wonder

One hundred years ago, the world stood dazzled at a series of five photographs of real-life fairies posing with two young girls. Elsie was 16 years old and Frances was nine. They took the photos to prove to their mothers that pixies were to blame for coming home wet and muddy after playing in a nearby Cottingley, England, stream.

The images of the delicate Cottingley Fairies are hauntingly beautiful. The first photo was taken in 1917, and they were eventually published alongside an article by Sir Arthur Conan Doyle (of Sherlock Holmes fame) in the Christmas 1920 edition of *The Strand Magazine*.

"The recognition of (the fairies') existence," Doyle concluded, "will jolt the material twentieth-century mind out of its heavy ruts in the mud, and will make it admit that there is a glamour and mystery to life."

·····>

·····>

Doyle's trust was misplaced. In 1983 the aged cousins confessed they had faked the photos. But Doyle's assessment of there being a "glamour and mystery to life" is spot on.

We are spiritual beings. Scripture tells us we are created just a little lower than the angels (Psalm 8:5) and that God formed us with the spark of eternity in our hearts (Ecclesiastes 3:11). We can't help it; we crave to witness, experience, and be dazzled by the miracles our souls sense all around us.

But to recognize wonder, you must know what you're looking at. We read about this in Acts 3, when Peter heals a lame beggar: "When all the people saw him walking and praising God, they recognized him as the same man who used to sit begging at the temple gate called Beautiful, and they were filled with wonder and amazement at what had happened to him" (verses 9-10 NIV).

The Cottingley Fairies, public domain in the United States.

The people were filled with wonder because they recognized God's work.

But it's easy to lose our wonder. Have you gotten so distracted by this frenzied life that you're not watching for God's presence? Are you so caught up in the busyness of the Christmas season that you haven't paused for the divine moments happening all around you? Do you even expect for those moments to happen at all?

I encourage you to stop and take a deep breath. Right now. Think back to that moment you first received your salvation. Remember, recognize, and receive the wonder and amazement of who God is and what He's done for you. Close your eyes and imagine the scene of a virgin mother cradling her baby—a child simultaneously human and Creator of the Universe.

I believe you'll see God's wonders all around you by starting with the wonders of His love.

Born thy people to deliver,
Born a child and yet a King,
Born to reign in us forever,
Now thy gracious kingdom bring.

"COME THOU LONG EXPECTED JESUS"
BY CHARLES WESLEY

DEC 7

Don't Miss Jesus

In 1933, an aspiring young dancer arrived at the Metro-Goldwyn-Mayer studio for his first screen test, hoping to get his big break. He poured his heart into the audition, but MGM's talent head, Burt Grady, was not impressed.

His memo said: "Fred Astaire. Can't act. Slightly bald. Can dance a little."

Fred Astaire, as you know, did end up a star. He dazzled in iconic films such as *Easter Parade*, *Funny Face*, and *Shall We Dance*, and his fancy footwork created iconic dance numbers for "Cheek to Cheek" in *Top Hat*, "Pick Yourself Up" in *Swing Time*, and "Puttin' On the Ritz" in *Blue Skies*. Fred Astaire and Ginger Rogers went on to become one of the biggest money-making teams in movie history.

Imagine looking right at the answer to all your troubles and completely missing it.

Israel had the same problem. God's chosen people spent centuries being overtaken by one empire or another, forced to move, and move again. Now they were under the oppressive Romans. There was hope, however: prophets foretold of a coming Messiah!

"Rejoice greatly, Daughter Zion!
·····>

Shout, Daughter Jerusalem! See, your king comes to you, righteous and victorious" (Zechariah 9:9a NIV).

The problem is, they missed the point. Israel wanted a royal king; they craved a conquering avenger who would liberate them from gentile oppression while riding on a gallant white steed.

Israel wanted a political conqueror. God, however, wanted to conquer their hearts. So, when a carpenter from Nazareth who—rumor had it—was born in a barn started shooting His mouth off about the Kingdom of God, the Jews weren't impressed.

The Old and New Testament refer to Jesus as the chief cornerstone that the builders rejected. And I like how Bob Farrell and Greg Nelson describe Israel's reaction to Jesus in their 1994 oratorio, *Saviour*: "Redemption did not come as they expected, for He came not as a king, nor as a thing of beauty that they should desire Him."

They missed Jesus.

It is tragic, heartbreaking, and exasperating that God's ultimate act of love—the pouring out and sacrifice of His only Son—would be met with such indifference, let alone violent outrage. And yet...

How many times have I treated Jesus as a security blanket, talisman, or magical genie who exists to grant my wishes? How often do I neglect to stay in communion with Him throughout the day and thank Him for every blessing? How often do I only think of Him when I find myself in trouble?

It's Christmas. Our King has been born! Let us embrace Jesus for what He is: The Savior of our lives, the desire of our souls, and the lover of our hearts. Don't miss Jesus!

When the angels had returned to heaven, the shepherds said to each other, "Let's go to Bethlehem! Let's see this thing that has happened, which the Lord has told us about."

LUKE 2:15 NLT

DEC 8

Standing on Holy Ground

I remember the first time I stepped onto the stage of Carnegie Hall in New York City. It was February 2019, and my dad was a guest conductor. I snuck into his choir.

The experience was absolutely surreal. Walking from the wings and through the stage doors, the first place your eyes go is up. And up, and up. Stern Auditorium (Carnegie's main venue) is a 2,804-seat quadruple-balconied cavern that soars five stories high. But the sheer size of the space is dwarfed by the history the room holds.

Since it opened in 1891, Carnegie Hall has hosted concerts for the most iconic names in every musical genre: Bob Dylan, Ella Fitzgerald, George Gershwin, Jay-Z, Judy Garland, Lady Gaga, Leonard Bernstein, Lin-Manuel Miranda, Luciano Pavarotti, Simon and Garfunkel, Sutton Foster, Tchaikovsky, The Beatles, Tony Bennett, Yo-Yo Ma… The list goes on.

The room feels almost sacred. Walking onto that hallowed hardwood in my off-the-rack discount tuxedo, I was astonished to think that I was about to sing on the same stage as one of my biggest musical heroes: Frank Sinatra. I didn't feel worthy to be walking on that "holy ground."

I wonder if that's how the shepherds felt as they entered the stable the night of Jesus's birth. I wonder if they realized they were walking on holy ground.

·····>

· · · · >

Because of their job, shepherds were dirty, smelly outcasts of Jewish society. By inviting these men to see His Son first, God was making a clear and powerful statement: "*All* are welcome in My Kingdom."

It was foreshadowing of things to come.

Thirty-three years later, as Jesus hung dying on the cross, the curtain that divided the people from the most holy place of the temple—the curtain that separated you and me from God—ripped in two.

Paul explains this in his letter to the Hebrews: Because of the blood of Jesus, we are invited to come into the most holy sanctuary in the heavenly realm boldly and without hesitation. For just as the veil was torn in two, Jesus's body was torn open to welcome us into God's house (adapted from Hebrews 10:19-21 TPT).

Just as the shepherds entering that stable were unworthy outsiders entering the nursery of a King, we are sinners welcomed into the Holy of Holies. And you don't have to travel far to get there: if you've accepted Jesus as your Savior, you "are the temple of the living God" (from 2 Corinthians 6:16).

Step with confidence onto this holy, hallowed ground and celebrate the newborn king. You've been invited.

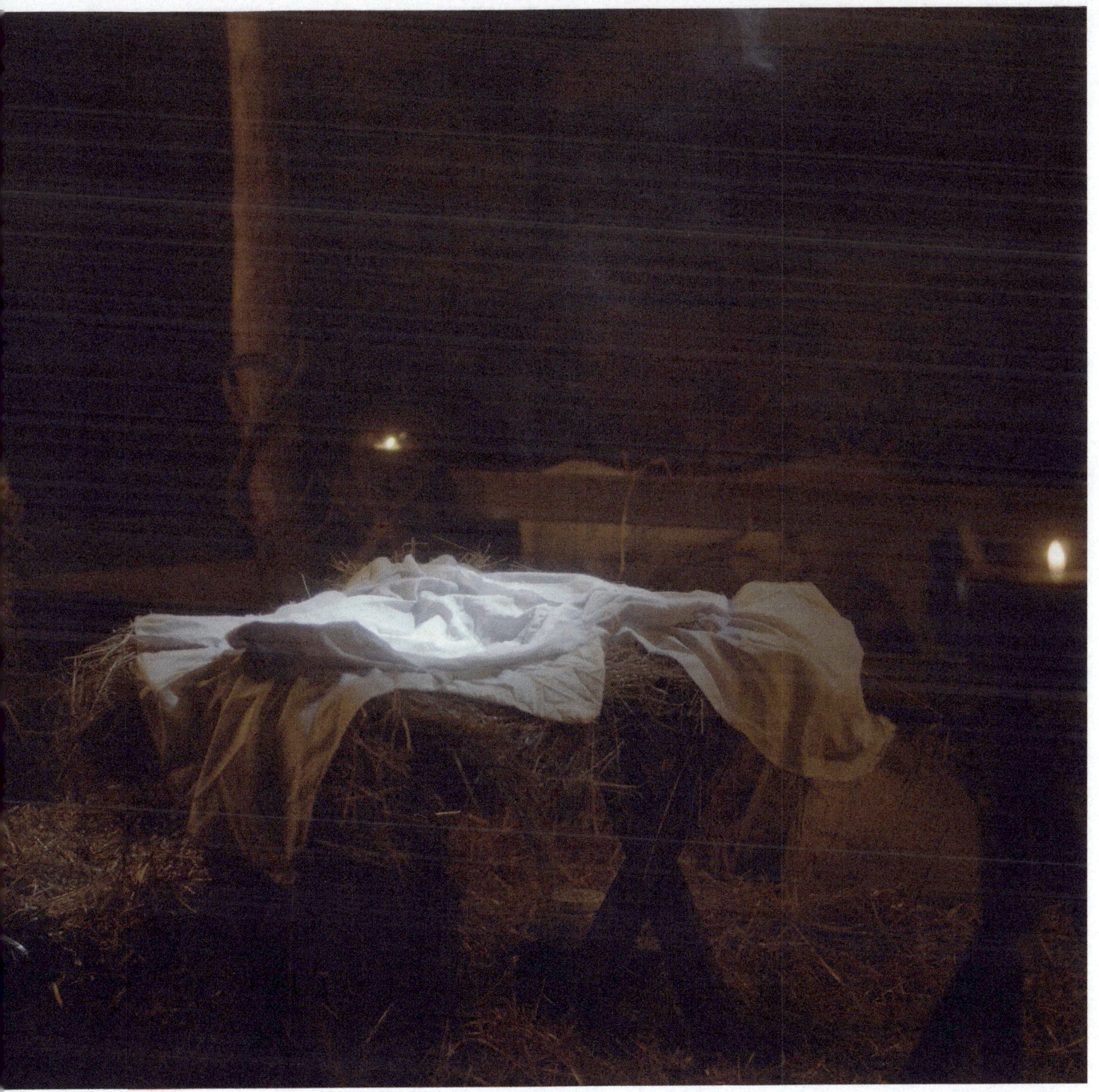

Seeing isn't believing. Believing is seeing.
JUDY THE ELF IN *THE SANTA CLAUSE*

Have You Ever Seen a Reindeer Fly?

I love Christmas movies. *A Charlie Brown Christmas, Home Alone, Elf, White Christmas*... I watch as many as I can each year. But my absolute favorite is 1994's *The Santa Clause*.

One of the best scenes happens midway through the movie. Neil, a psychiatrist, is trying to discourage his young stepson's belief that his dad is Santa.

"Charlie, it's just not logical," Neil says, holding a figurine of Santa next to a large globe. "How can one man, in one night, visit all the children of the world?"

Charlie fends off his questions until Neil finally asks, "What about the reindeer? Have you ever seen a reindeer fly?"

"Yes," Charlie answers. "Well, I haven't," Neil fumbles back.

Charlie turns the question around: "Have you ever seen a million dollars?" Neil says no. Charlie replies, "Just because you haven't seen it doesn't mean it doesn't exist."

Oh, the truth this scene holds!

·····>

....>

Believing takes faith, a "confidence in what we hope for and assurance about what we do not see" (Hebrews 11:1 NIV). Faith is more than wishful thinking, and it's being confident of something you can't prove in court.

I'm reminded of the moment in Mark 9 where a father begs Jesus to cast an evil spirit out of his son. Jesus challenges the father's conviction: "Everything is possible for one who believes." The father exclaims, "I do believe; help me overcome my unbelief" (from verses 23-24 NIV).

I do believe. Help me overcome my unbelief. How many times have you prayed that prayer?

Faith is hard. Just ask Thomas. He refused to believe Jesus was alive despite reports from the other disciples. "I won't believe it unless I see the nail wounds in his hands, put my fingers into them, and place my hand into the wound in his side," he said (John 20:25b NLT).

Faith requires sacrifice, trust, and the release of what we previously knew to be true. That's why Jesus sent us the Holy Spirit to be a helper and advocate to testify to us (John 14:26-27) through our experiences in this world and by new truths revealed in the reading of ancient Scripture.

And let this encourage you: your faith will be rewarded. In John 20:29, Jesus says that "blessed are those who have not seen and yet have believed" (NIV).

We can believe the truths of our Lord and Savior Jesus Christ, not because we've touched his nail-pierced hands, but we've touched his nail-pierced hands because we believed!

Bubble Lights

Nestled in the garland I drape across my mantel at Christmas is a strand of bubble lights.

My Grandma Helen always made Christmases extra special for us young grandkids. Some of my warmest memories are at her and Grandpa's house Christmas night. And on their mantel—every year, without fail—was a string of bubble lights. Warm, glittering, effervescent. They were magical to me.

When Grandma died shortly before Christmas in 2018, I purchased my own string of bubble lights. No Christmas would ever be the same, and I wanted a tangible reminder of the importance she had in my life.

Maybe you, too, have found that Christmastime can be a painful reminder of a loved one's absence.

We pray the pain will go away. And though the intensity may ease over time, grief never fully dissipates. God didn't design us that way. Instead, grief remains as a dull ache in the back of our hearts, or unexpectedly washes over us in waves. Even Jesus, who had the power to raise the dead to life, wept over the death of a friend (John 11:32-36). Heartache is something we'll always endure this side of Heaven.

But praise God for His compassion, because He's hidden a blessing in it.

Christian theologian Dietrich Bonhoeffer wrote of grief, "To the extent the emptiness truly remains unfilled, one remains connected to the other person through it.... God in no way fills it but much more leaves it precisely unfilled and thus helps us preserve—even in pain—the authentic relationship. Further more, the more beautiful and full the remembrances, the more difficult the separation."

Read that again. Soak it in.

Bonhoeffer goes on to say that with gratitude, we are able to change the torment of memory into silent joy: "One bears what was lovely in the past not as a thorn, but as a precious gift deep within, a hidden treasure of which one can always be certain."

Memories of a loved one are living photographs pasted into the scrapbooks of our hearts.

I'm learning to find joy amid the sorrow for those I've lost. That person gave me something worth treasuring, and I'm grateful to them, and to God, for it. This propels me forward.

Each year as I hang those bubble lights on the mantel, big wet tears mix with uncontainable laughter. Grandma's influence in my life and the memories I have of her are an incredible gift. Until I hug her again in Heaven, I'll always miss her. That's OK. That's good.

And maybe someday my two daughters—or even their children many, many years from now—will think back to their earliest Christmases and fondly remember the bubble lights on the mantel.

✳ ✳ ✳

Yep, that's an authentic Vogel family artifact, circa 1994. This photo was taken on Christmas Day with my grandparents at their home with my younger brother (in the tiny rocking chair) and cousins. Most importantly, note the bubble lights on the mantel.

Jesus replied, "The Kingdom of God can't be detected by visible signs. You won't be able to say, 'Here it is!' or 'It's over there!' For the Kingdom of God is already among you."

LUKE 17:20b-21 NLT

Heaven Invades

My dad, brother, and I enjoy seeing each new Marvel movie together. For its part, Marvel seems content to give us plenty of opportunities to do so. Over the last 15 years of Marvel's "Cinematic Universe," I've observed plots shifting from super powers sourced from earthly technologies (think The Incredible Hulk, Iron Man, and Captain America) to interstellar and magical fantasy (like Thor, Shang-Chi, and the Eternals).

Now, one of the MCU's plot obsessions is the "multiverse," the idea that there are parallel realities running simultaneously to ours, obscured by the dimensions of our own universe. When there's a great cosmic disturbance (I'm looking at you, Dr. Strange), these parallel universes can collide, allowing one to cross over into another.

It sounds fantastical, but it's real. And it's in the Bible.

In Luke 2, we read of some tired shepherds who are out in the quiet, darkened fields, minding their own business and keeping an eye on the sheep. Out of nowhere, a "company of the heavenly host" appeared, singing praises to God (Luke 2:13-14).

When Jesus arrived on Earth, a great cosmic event occurred.

·····>

·····>

God, Himself, was now living as a human among us. Heaven invaded, breaking through our dim reality. It opened a portal to Heaven that revealed hundreds of dazzling angels announcing this incredible news. And our world would never be the same again.

Jesus came, and He brought Heaven with Him. That's right, Heaven is here with us right now. It's right in front of us, we just can't quite see it.

In NASA's Apollo missions, the walls of the lunar module—the contraption that landed astronauts on the moon—were essentially a layer of foil just over .3 millimeters thick. The jab of a sharp pencil was all it would take to introduce the astronauts inside to the majesty (and life-sucking vacuum) of space outside.

That's a bit how I imagine our separation from the reality of the presence of Heaven among us; a thin veil that's barely separating us from the other side.

As we each go through life, especially during this Christmas season, keep that in mind. Heaven has invaded earth! You're probably bumping into angels and rubbing elbows with saints right now. The Kingdom of God is already here, and if you're a follower of Jesus, you're living in it. Look forward to the day you get to see it!

> You may ask, "How did this tradition get started?" I'll tell you... I don't know. But it's a tradition, and because of our traditions, every one of us knows who he is and what God expects him to do.
>
> **TEVYE IN *FIDDLER ON THE ROOF***

DEC 12

✦ ✧ ✦

Christmas Traditions

I grew up in a small church that is part of the Mennonite Brethren denomination. Many there are direct descendants of German immigrants. At Christmas, one beloved tradition is singing the carol, "*Nun ist sie Erschienen.*"

Translated "The Sun Has Now Risen," the hymn was written in 1884 by Wilhelm Horn (tune by James R. Murray), and was a favorite of German-Russian Mennonites arriving in America during that era. The music is joyous and bright, the words are pure celebration.

In the more than 130 years since, Mennonite congregations continue to sing this beautiful carol. Enjoy this gem from a 2019 bulletin plucked from a small church not far from where I grew up: "'*Nun ist sie Erschienen*' harkens back from when one-room school houses in the area each had an annual Christmas Eve program. This hymn was often sung at the program by everyone in attendance. We continue this tradition. You are welcome to sing the hymn in English or German."

In my own church, on Christmas Eve night, it was absolutely stunning to hear each voice singing "*Nun ist sie Erschienen*"

·····>

together, in a language many didn't understand, in celebration of Jesus's birth and in tribute to the legacy of generations present.

I'm sure you have your own favorite Christmas traditions. Maybe it's caroling door-to-door, or decorating sugar cookies, or going to Grandma's after the Christmas Eve service. To some (me), a small paper bag filled with peanuts, chocolates, and an orange provokes a surplus of sentimental post-pageant joy.

Traditions help us remember and honor our families and heritage. And when filled with purpose and meaning, traditions are a wonderful gift from God.

First, traditions remind us of the blessings and faithfulness of God. The psalmist writes, "I will remember the deeds of the Lord; yes, I will remember your miracles of long ago" (Psalm 77:11 NIV).

Second, traditions guide us into the future. As the Israelites entered the Promised Land, Moses instructed them to "remember the days of old; consider the generations long past. Ask your father and he will tell you, your elders, and they will explain to you" (Deuteronomy 32:7 NIV).

And finally, traditions help us realign our contemporary lives with the Truth of Jesus: "And he took bread, and when he had given thanks, he broke it and gave it to them, saying, 'This is my body, which is given for you. Do this in *remembrance of me*'" (Luke 22:19 ESV, emphasis mine).

Cherish your Christmas traditions. Practice them with joy and delight. As you do, remember why: "Through faith in the Savior comes peace and salvation. Sing with joy, all you ransomed, the Savior is born!"

The Sun Has Now Risen

(NUN IST SIE ERSCHIENEN,
TRANSLATED BY P. C. HIEBERT)

WORDS BY WILHELM HORN
MUSIC BY JAMES R. MURRAY

The sun has now risen in heavenly glory,
And shines through the darkness of night;
Now rejoice and sing praises, yea, shout the glad story,
For in Christ the Redeemer is healing and light.

REFRAIN:
To God be the glory, and goodwill to men;
Through Christ our Redeemer shall peace come again.

The world lay benighted in death and destruction,
All mankind in sin was forlorn;
But through faith in the Savior comes peace and salvation,
Sing with joy, all you ransomed, the Savior is born.

I encourage you to listen to this beautiful arrangement:
youtu.be/3UY89bJZ4CY

The Joy of Christmas

The word "joy" and the Christmas season are inseparable. You see it printed, painted, penned, carved, or sewn onto signs, decor, mugs, pillows, and greeting cards. It's plastered up and down the aisles of Hobby Lobby. (I should know; I spend a lot of time in Hobby Lobby at Christmastime.)

We associate joy with Christmas because it is such a central theme of the nativity story. John the Baptist leaped for *joy* in his mother's womb at the news of Jesus's coming. The angel brought the shepherds good tidings of great *joy*. Mary glorified the Lord and *rejoiced* in her Savior. The Magi were *overjoyed* when they arrived at His home.

This joy that we read about is more than just celebration or pleasure. It's a quenching of a thirst for salvation deep within us.

In his book *Soul Keeping*, John Ortberg writes that our souls require a center to give them identity, purpose, hope, and foundation. He says that when we center our souls on something other than God's salvation, they crave that false idol all the more. Like an addict who discovers that the more drugs he uses, the more drugs he needs, trying to satisfy your soul with anything but Jesus only compounds the deadly craving.

·····>

•••>

"Our ceaseless craving for more, though it can kill us when unredeemed, may be a hint of the joy that we were made for when the soul finds its center in God," Ortberg writes.

Jesus's arrival on earth was the beginning of the end of our souls' cravings for salvation. It doesn't matter the mistakes you've made or the hurtful words you've said or the regrets you play over and over in your mind. Jesus wants to be your Savior. When Jesus redeemed you from your sins on the cross, your soul was filled and made whole.

In the musical *Wicked*, Glinda poignantly realizes that "happy is what happens when all your dreams come true." Christmas is the moment your soul's dreams came true. Christmas is the moment your soul realized its worth.

Isaiah 35:10 says, "Those who have been ransomed by the Lord… will enter Jerusalem singing, crowned with everlasting joy. Sorrow and mourning will disappear, and they will be filled with joy and gladness" (NLT).

Your soul was made to experience pure, ecstatic, ceaseless, and unspeakable joy; it is just waiting for a Savior to redeem it.

Well, it's Christmas, and that Savior has come!

O Zion, that bringest good tidings, get thee up into the high mountain; O Jerusalem, that bringest good tidings, lift up thy voice with strength; lift it up, be not afraid; say unto the cities of Judah, Behold your God!

ISAIAH 40:9 KJV

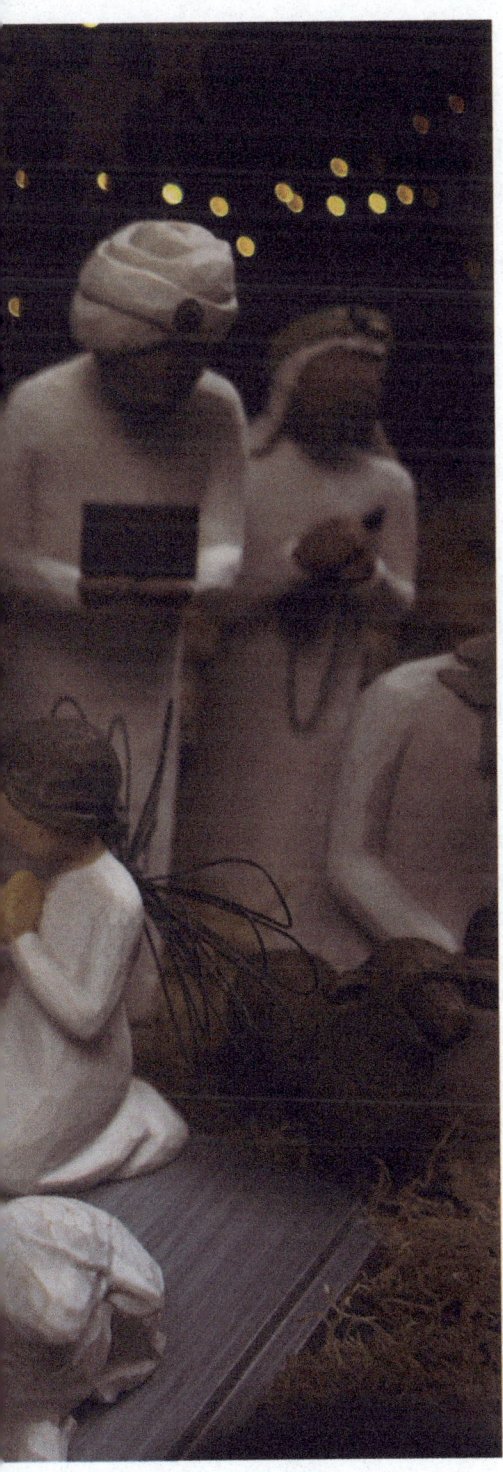

DEC 14

And His Name Shall Be Called...

George Frideric Handel's *Messiah* is one of the most well-known and oft-performed choral works in Western music. From the opening strains of "Comfort ye, my people" to the jubilant "Hallelujah Chorus" and crescendoing to the triumphant finale of "Amen!," the oratorio blends the prophesies, life, death, resurrection, and second coming of Jesus into one immortal musical masterpiece.

I've had the opportunity to sing in 11 productions of *Messiah*—enjoying it from the audience at least a dozen times more—and each happened in early December, on the threshold of Christmas. For me, Christmas and the music of Handel's *Messiah* will forever be linked.

Near the middle of the first of *Messiah*'s three parts is a sparkling setting of the Isaiah 9:6 prophecy:

For unto us a child is born, unto us a son is given:

·····>

and the government shall be upon his shoulder; and his name shall be called Wonderful Counsellor, The Mighty God, The Everlasting Father, The Prince of Peace.

I will never be able to read this verse without singing it in my head. (Or, for that matter, out loud.) Jesus has been given many names: Bread of Life, King of Kings, High Priest, Chief Cornerstone, Good Shepherd, Alpha and Omega... The list goes on. But perhaps none are as iconic as these four bestowed upon Him by Isaiah.

The Wonderful Counselor. Jesus is full of wonder—wonder-*full*—and overflowing with truths too dazzling for us to fully understand. He counsels us not like a good therapist, but as a caring shepherd who guides our hearts back to their Creator and rekindles the spark of eternity in our souls.

The Mighty God. Jesus is simultaneously Son of God and God Himself. Like the infinite galaxies that exist in the vastness of space, I know it to be true, but I cannot comprehend it. He created the universe with a word, defeated death by death, and holds the future in His hands.

The Everlasting Father. Jesus is the architect of eternity. Through Him was created all space and time, from Him was conceived mankind, and by Him we are born again into eternal paradise. He exists in infinity, yet offers us the tangible, tender relationship of a dad.

The Prince of Peace. Jesus's earthly life was met with confrontation, controversy, and cruelty. His entire being, however, is saturated by serenity and compassion. Like a prince sharing wealth with a pauper, Jesus confers His peace to those who abide in His law and love.

Thank you, Jesus, for Your counsel, Your might, Your love, and Your peace.

DEC 15

 Stealing Christmas

"**Every Who down in Whoville** liked Christmas a lot. But the Grinch, who lived just north of Whoville, did not!"

We're not exactly sure what the Grinch has against the most wonderful time of the year. Maybe his shoes are too tight or his head isn't screwed on quite right. But whatever the reason, he can't stand it.

"Why, for 53 years I've put up with it now," he says. "I must stop Christmas from coming... But how?"

Occasionally, it can feel like the Grinch won: like he snuck down Mount Crumpit and into your house, stuffed your joy in a bag, gobbled up your roast beast, and made off like a bandit.

Maybe you've lost a job or are buried in a financial pit. Maybe you are estranged from a child or recently buried your spouse. Maybe you're facing debilitating pain or just got devastating news from your doctor. Maybe you're fighting depression, anxiety, or hopelessness. This time of year, when the whole world seems so blissfully joyous, your sorrow intensifies tenfold.

But I want to encourage you with this: nothing—*nothing!*—can stop Christmas from coming.

·····>

....>

Satan's number one tactic is to make a person feel separated from God and from God's people. It's his nasty way of bringing a little hell to earth. He'll throw obstacles in your path and spit lies in your face. He'll even twist your sense of direction until up is down and right is wrong. But it's all smoke and mirrors. What Satan doesn't want you to know is that he can't actually keep you from God.

God's love is relentless. He sent Jesus to this world to claim the keys to death and destruction. There is nothing you can do, nothing you can say, and nowhere you can go that He won't find you, accept you, and love you.

Psalm 139:7-8 says it all: "I can never escape from your Spirit! I can never get away from your presence! If I go up to heaven, you are there; if I go down to the grave, you are there" (NLT).

Satan can't steal your joy, but God *can* use suffering to increase it. (Read Romans 5:3-5.)

Satan can't separate you from Jesus; God's love is too far-reaching. (Read Romans 8:38-39.)

And Satan can't void the promises of God; His Word is Living Truth. (Read Isaiah 55:10-11.)

Ever since the serpent's deceit caused Adam and Eve to sin, God's rescue plan has been in action to restore creation—to restore *you*—to Himself. Take heart: "The God of peace will soon crush Satan under your feet" (Romans 16:20a NIV).

If life seems to be crumbling all around you, remember that Jesus is victorious. God loves you. And nothing can stop Christmas from coming.

Everyone who lights the candles has a bit of ancient spark. We are miracles, lighting up the dark.

**"WE ARE LIGHTS"
BY STEVE YOUNG
& STEPHEN SCHWARTZ**

DEC 16

Turn Off the Dark

In June 2011, one of the most expensive and technically-complex musicals ever produced opened on Broadway, giving Marvel's web-slinging hero his Great White Way debut. It was called *Spider-Man: Turn Off the Dark*.

The doomed production is all but forgotten: it closed less than three years later at a financial loss, plagued by record-setting delays, poor reviews, and frequent cast injuries.

Yet, the title has stuck with me: *Turn Off the Dark*.

Darkness is the default. Without intervention, everything we see and know is shrouded in black. We have to turn off the dark by turning *on* the light.

Sin is the same way. Since the fall of Adam and Eve, sin is the default setting of our world. It separates us from God, and without intervention we are lost in the darkness of our own inequity.

Jesus's birth changed all that. Isaiah prophesied of His birth that "the people who walked in darkness have seen a great light; those who dwelt in the land of the shadow of death, upon them a light has shined" (9:2 NKJV).

Jesus came to bring salvation, and

·····>

·····>

He even said, "I am the light of the world. Whoever follows me will not walk in darkness, but will have the light of life" (John 8:12 ESV).

Here's the really cool thing about light: it's contagious. For instance, the moon doesn't make its own light. It reflects the sun. But even though it's not making light itself, the moon still glows brightly down on us at night.

In the same way, Jesus says that when we remain in His light, we *become* the light (John 12:36). Translation: when we walk with Jesus, we reflect His light and turn into light sources for others. We become the light of the world (Matthew 5:14)!

There's a beautiful song for this season by lyricist Steve Young and composer Stephen Schwartz (*Godspell, Wicked, Prince of Egypt,* and others) called "We Are Lights." In its chorus is this powerful, poignant phrase:

> *We are glowing, growing miracles*
> *We are lights, shining on and on*

Jesus came to earth by the light of a dazzling star and ascended back to Heaven in the brilliance of a blue sky. Light was and is in everything He does, and He imparts the gift of the blazing Holy Spirit into each of our hearts. Let us reflect His light to turn off the dark of this world.

Finding Jesus

On April 12, 1961, Soviet cosmonaut Yuri Gagarin became the first human to escape the gravitational bindings of Earth when he completed a single orbit around our planet. His cramped *Vostok 1* capsule shot around the earth at 17,500 miles per hour before bringing the hero safely home.

Hurtling through space, Gagarin peered out of his small porthole, searching the endless universe for something he was certain would be there. But alas...

"I looked and looked and looked," Gagarin said after he returned, "but I didn't see God."✛

Two thousand years earlier, the people of Israel had the same problem.

·····>

✛Full disclosure: Several variations of this quote exist, as well as the claim that it was actually then-Soviet Premier Nikita Khrushchev who said during a speech about the Soviet's anti-religion campaign, "Gagarin flew into space, but didn't see any god there."

Prophets foretold Jesus's arrival for thousands of years. But Israel was so focused on where *they* wanted the Messiah to be, they looked past where He really was. They expected their King to arrive in a chariot and reign from the splendor of a royal palace. But their Savior was born to poor parents in a cold, dirty barn.

Jesus always shows up where the culture least expects Him. Hobnobbing with the religious leaders? Abiding strictly to the religious law? Nope. He's hanging out with prostitutes and tax collectors, showing them God's compassion. Being served from a golden platter? Nope. He's on His knees, washing His friends' dirty feet to demonstrate the heart of a servant.

Today, you wouldn't find Jesus flattering the preacher who packs a 10,000-seat auditorium; He's strengthening the tired volunteer at the homeless shelter, showing

He will leave the 99 to help the one. And Jesus doesn't just love the man who takes his family to church, or the woman who shines God's light in her workplace. He also loves the person who struggles in their sexual identity, the woman who had an abortion, the teen who tried to commit suicide. The adulterer, the murderer, the glutton, the addict, the depressed, the hopeless, the unwanted.

I don't know what Yuri Gagarin expected to find from his spaceship. But he was looking for Jesus in all the wrong places. The King of Heaven will always show up where He doesn't make sense because His kind of love doesn't make sense. We look for Him in the stars, but we'll also find Him in the gutter, where He invites us to join Him as His ambassadors.

Jesus rules the world with truth and grace, and He makes the nations prove the glories of His righteousness. But not on *our* terms. The Messiah came with ambitions more glorious than our earthly expectations.

Look for Jesus where you least expect Him. He'll be there.

Christmas snow can never disappear completely. It sometimes goes away for almost a year at a time and takes the form of spring and summer rain. But you can bet your boots that when a good, jolly December wind kisses it, it will turn into Christmas snow all over again!

SANTA CLAUS IN FROSTY THE SNOWMAN

White as Snow

I find nothing more peaceful than to stand alone on a windless, snowing night. The scenery is a serene, smooth monochrome accented only by sparkling streetlight. And it's quiet: the veil of falling snow insulates you from the surrounding world. The only sound—if not actually imagined—is the soft *pfff* of each flake touching the ground.

Snow is inexplicably linked to Christmas. I think Irving Berlin accidentally did it with his 1942 song "White Christmas." It conjures an old-fashioned nostalgia that automatically associates snow with the holiday season.

(To prove my point: almost every other Christmas song that centers around snow was written *after* "White Christmas": "I'll Be Home for Christmas" in 1943, "Let It Snow" in 1945, "Sleigh Ride" in 1948, "Marshmallow World" in 1949, "Frosty the Snowman" and "Silver Bells" in 1950, and "It's Beginning to Look a Lot Like Christmas" in 1951. The only exceptions are "Jingle Bells" and "Winter Wonderland"—1857 and 1934, respectively—but they were not originally intended to be Christmassy.)

However, I think there's another, better, reason why Christmas and snow go together. And it's biblical:

"Come now, let us settle the matter," God said through His prophet. "Though your sins are like scarlet, they shall be as white as snow; though they are red as crimson, they shall be like wool" (Isaiah 1:18 NIV).

This was God making a promise.

The Old Testament practice of sacrificing an innocent animal was a sign that you were restoring your relationship with God. Like the blood of the lambs that covered doorways to redeem Israelite families the night of Passover in Egypt, the sacrifice of blood covered your sin. But it was only temporary. As soon you sinned again, back to the altar you went.

Paul wrote to the Hebrews, "Nearly everything under the law was purified with blood, since forgiveness only comes through an outpouring of blood" (Hebrews 9:22 TPT).

It was an imperfect system, but one that pointed to God's ultimate solution. Jesus, God's one and only Son, was the spotless Lamb (John 1:29) who was to be the final sacrifice for our sins (Hebrews 10:10).

Jesus's blood doesn't just cover over our sins, but completely washes them away. Once painted red as crimson by the fading blood of an animal, we are now washed white as snow by the eternal blood of Jesus.

Just as a winter snow cleanses the ground and purifies the air, Jesus cleanses our sins and purifies our souls. As snow brings beauty to God's creation, Jesus brings His beautiful creation back to God.

For Christ is born of Mary,
And, gathered all above
While mortals sleep, the angels keep
Their watch of wond'ring love.

"O LITTLE TOWN OF BETHLEHEM" BY PHILLIPS BROOKS

DEC 19

The Wonders of His Love

You've heard the phrase, "good things come in small packages." Many things we consider valuable are small: diamonds, rare coins, a first-edition book, or the 1952 Mickey Mantle baseball card that sold in August 2022 for a record-breaking $12.6 million.

This idea that an insignificant-looking item can have immeasurable value is at the very bedrock of the Christmas story.

In C. S. Lewis's final Narnia novel, *The Last Battle*, we find Tirian—descendant of King Caspian X and the final king of Narnia—entering an ancient stable. But he's taken aback when the inside of the shack turns out to be a vast, grassy countryside with a brilliant blue sky. He has entered Aslan's country.

"It seems, then," said Tirian, smiling himself, "that the Stable seen from within and the Stable seen from without are two different places."

"Yes," said the Lord Digory. "Its inside is bigger than its outside."

·····>

·····>

"Yes," said Queen Lucy. "In our world too, a Stable once had something inside it that was bigger than our whole world."

I love that last line!

Inside a small, unassuming Bethlehem barn was a baby laying in a manger. But that humble, helpless baby was the King of the Universe, the Lord of Life, and the Embodiment of Love... a love greater than anyone could have asked for or imagined.

First John 4:9-10 says, "This is how God showed his love among us: He sent his one and only Son into the world that we might live through him. This is love: not that we loved God, but that he loved us and sent his Son as an atoning sacrifice for our sins" (NIV).

God's love is not a verb, it's a noun. God doesn't just love, He *is* love. Love is God's very being. He dwells in our hearts so that we can know and experience His love. His love surpasses anything we could ever hope to understand in this world. Surrounded by His love, we are "filled with all the fullness of God" (Ephesians 3:19).

The stable seen from the outside—small, dark, and ordinary—was different than the stable seen from the inside. It was filled with love: alive, boundless, infinite love that grows and flows in us: "Those who are loved by God, let his love continually pour from you to one another, because God is love" (1 John 4:7 TPT).

This is the wonder of God's love! Let us marvel at and celebrate the love that was born in a small stable; a love that is bigger than our whole world.

God's kingdom is already among you.

LUKE 17:21B MSG

DEC 20

✷ A Little Bit of Heaven

The stillness of night covered the town of Bethlehem. The streets, which a few hours earlier had been bustling with families arriving from out of town for the governor's census, were quiet and deserted. If you listened closely, you might hear the echo of angelic singing coming from the grazing fields outside of town. And hundreds of miles to the east, a handful of stargazers were just noticing something different in the sky.

The windows of every Bethlehem home, shop, and guesthouse were dim; the only light to be seen was from the stars above. Except... The doorway of a small stable behind an innkeeper's quarters is lit with the soft glow of a lantern. The hush of the evening is interrupted by the coo of a baby.

While the city slept, something amazing happened. Heaven came to the earth.

You and I probably share a similar imagining of Heaven. Golden streets, brilliant light, lush fruit trees, maybe a couple harps, and pure happiness on the face of every soul you meet. But what makes Heaven paradise is not the scenery or the menu. Heaven is paradise because God is there.

I'm excited to go to Heaven. In fact, I've often found myself feeling homesick for it. But I recently

·····>

realized something. The best part of Heaven is already here: God's presence.

John the Baptist recognized this. He preached, "Repent! For the Kingdom of Heaven is near" (Matthew 3:1 NIV). And Jesus tried to tell us this. "It's not something that can be observed," He said, "because the Kingdom of God is already in your midst" (from Luke 17:21).

Heaven isn't a place; Heaven is the presence of God. And Jesus isn't just God's Son; Jesus *is* God walking on Earth in a human body.

Heaven came to Earth on that quiet night in Bethlehem. And then it stayed.

"My Father will send you a Helper," Jesus told His followers, "and He will stay with you forever" (from John 14:16).

Though Jesus ascended into the clouds, He left behind the Holy Spirit. If you have put your faith in Jesus, your body is a temple that the Holy Spirit—that is, the presence of God—dwells within (1 Corinthians 6:19).

Heaven is not a magical place in the sky. And it's not just a destination for the future. Heaven has come to Earth.

And a little bit of Heaven rests in you.

I just don't understand Christmas, I guess. I like getting presents and sending Christmas cards and decorating trees and all that, but I'm still not happy.

CHARLIE BROWN IN A CHARLIE BROWN CHRISTMAS

DEC 21

A Little Love

I remember watching *A Charlie Brown Christmas* every year as far back as my memory goes. It's one of my most beloved traditions. Now, my daughters ask for it by name.

You know the story: Charlie Brown is depressed. "I think there must be something wrong with me," he tells Linus. "Christmas is coming, but I'm not happy."

Charlie Brown is distracted by the over-commercialization of the Christmas season. He's become cynical, disillusioned, and depressed. Given the task of finding the tree for a Christmas pageant, Charlie Brown is drawn to a frail, spindly sapling that seems to reflect his own fragility.

"I don't know, Charlie Brown," Linus warns. "This doesn't seem to fit the modern spirit."

Linus is right. Laughter erupts from the other kids when the tree is brought in, and Charlie Brown snaps. "Isn't there anyone who knows what Christmas is all about?"

There's a pause.

"Sure, Charlie Brown," Linus says. "I can tell you what Christmas is all about."

·····>

As the auditorium dims, Linus steps into a spotlight and recites the Christmas story.

"And there were in the same country shepherds abiding in the field, keeping watch over their flock by night. And lo, the angel of the Lord came upon them, and the glory of the Lord shone round about them: and they were sore afraid. And the angel said unto them, 'Fear not: for behold, I bring unto you good tidings of great joy, which shall be to all people. For unto you is born this day in the City of David a Savior, which is Christ the Lord. And this shall be a sign unto you; Ye shall find the babe wrapped in swaddling clothes, lying in a manger.' And suddenly there was with the angel a multitude of the heavenly host, praising God, and saying, 'Glory to God in the highest, and on earth peace, good will toward men'" (Luke 2:8-14 KJV).

I'm baffled they still let this play on primetime network TV, but I'm glad they do. I love this moment. The frivolity of Snoopy, the materialism of Lucy, and the cynicism of Charlie Brown fade away as the profound truth of Christmas is stated simply and sweetly.

God sent His Son into the world to save it by His love.

Later, as he gently wraps his blue blanket around the base of Charlie Brown's tree, Linus makes an observation: "I never thought it was such a bad little tree. It's not bad at all, really. Maybe it just needs a little love."

Do you know someone who is struggling through this Christmas season? Share the love of Jesus with them. Or maybe that someone is you. Know that you are loved.

Linus said it before The Beatles did: all we need is a little love.

DEC 22

Treasures of the Heart

I remember the moments I first held each of my daughters. There was a tiny, helpless baby cradled in my arms. I looked into her face; we had only met moments before, yet I felt like I had known her forever. I felt a type of love I had never experienced before. I was a new dad—feeling ridiculously proud, fiercely protective, and wildly unprepared.

I remember thinking, *I wish I could capture this moment and keep it forever. I wish I could hold it in my hand and roll it over and over to re-experience this miracle.*

Those moments gave me a new appreciation for this short phrase tucked quietly into the account of Jesus's birth: "Mary treasured up all these things and pondered them in her heart" (Luke 2:19 NIV).

Mary has just given birth to her first child. Add to that the baby's conception was announced by an angel, her child is the Son of God, a brilliant star is beaming a spotlight over them, a rowdy bunch of shepherds just barged in to worship Him, and they were saying something about *more* angels.

There, in this joyous chaos, I imagine Mary resting on some

·····>

hay. As she cradles Jesus, she tries to capture every moment, every word, and every emotion to tuck away as treasure in her heart; treasure to cherish the rest of her life.

Mary was preparing her heart. Have you prepared yours?

In the carol "Joy to the World," I imagine hymn writer Isaac Watts had the unprepared innkeeper in mind when he penned the words, "let every heart prepare Him room."

The inn was already crowded to capacity by the time Mary and Joseph arrived in Bethlehem, and the innkeeper had failed to prepare a place for them. (Though, without any record that an angel appeared to him as well, I suppose we can't fault him.)

It's impossible to have an empty heart. If you don't intentionally set aside space for Jesus, it will become crowded with other things. These could be earthly idols like money, possessions, or status. They could be hidden corrosives like hatred, spite, deceit, or greed. Or they could even be good things that you've misplaced above Jesus, like family, volunteering, generosity, or self-care.

Jesus warned us that "wherever your treasure is, there the desires of your heart will be" (Matthew 6:21).

What are you treasuring? As we approach Christmas Day, make sure you're preparing room in your time and in your soul to ponder the joy of this celebration. Prepare your heart for Jesus.

Those who are loved by God, let his love continually pour from you to one another, because God is love. Everyone who loves is fathered by God and experiences an intimate knowledge of him.

1 JOHN 4:7 TPT

DEC
23

Give a Bit of Love to the World

Walt Disney was quite fond of Robert and Richard Sherman, the prolific songwriting siblings who penned the iconic tunes for his movies *Chitty Chitty Bang Bang*, *The Jungle Book*, and *Mary Poppins*, among others.

On Fridays, Walt would invite the brothers into his office above the studio.

"He'd say, 'Play it,'" Richard recalled in a documentary I watched recently. "And we knew he wanted to hear his favorite song."

As Walt gazed out his north window overlooking the entertainment empire he'd built from scratch, Robert and Richard would sit at the piano and play "Feed the Birds."

If you haven't recently, I encourage you to pull up the Julie Andrews recording and listen to it now. Close your eyes while you do. The music is beautifully hypnotizing, the words almost haunting.

·····▸

"Come feed the little birds, show them you care, and you'll be glad if you do." All it costs is "tuppence a bag."

"That song was Walt's credo," Richard said. "He loved the idea that it doesn't take much to give love, and that's what the song is all about. (Walt) was feeding the birds. He was giving a bit of love to the world all the time."

On a silent, holy night, God gave the ultimate love to the world.

"Do not be afraid," the angel told the startled shepherds. "I bring you good news that will cause great joy for all the people" (Luke 2:10).

Did you catch that? All the people. The whole world.

A Savior had been born! But what the Jews didn't understand was that the Messiah wasn't just for them. Their job was to take the love they received and go save the world.

First John 4:10-11 says, "This is love: not that we loved God, but that he loved us and sent his Son as an atoning sacrifice for our sins. Dear friends, since God so loved us, we also ought to love one another" (NIV).

Cut back to the film: as Mary Poppins shakes the snow globe, a woman sits on the steps of St. Paul's, selling bags of crumbs to feed the birds. "All around the cathedral, the saints and apostles look down as she sells her wares," the Sherman brothers wrote. "Although you can't see it, you know they are smiling each time someone shows that he cares."

Christmas is the incarnation of God. God is love. Love has been given to you. Now go share that love. This Christmas, give a bit of love to the world.

DEC 24

✸ Christmas Eve

Plans are made. Cards are written. Shopping is done. There's a bit more baking to do, perhaps a few more presents to wrap. But today is bursting with excitement, expectation, and joyful anticipation.

Today is Christmas Eve. Tomorrow is Christmas!

I love the quote on the previous page. Joe is describing his friend Yogi Berra: every day of his life is Christmas Eve. To me, that means he lived each day with anticipation for what tomorrow could bring; each day one step closer to the fulfillment of a promise.

With that in mind, consider this: Starting at the dawn of creation and until the night of Jesus's birth, *every day* was like Christmas Eve.

The Gospel of John begins with this statement: "In the beginning was the Word, and the Word was with God, and the Word was God. He was with God in the beginning" (John 1:1-2 NIV).

A bit later in verse 14, John makes this proclamation: "The Word became human and made his home among us (NLT). We have seen his glory, the glory of the one and only Son, who came from the Father, full of grace and truth" (NIV).

If Jesus is the Word, and the Word

·····>

was there at the beginning of time, then Jesus was part of God's plan to redeem His people from the very, very, very beginning. The Old and New Testaments are one continuous story of God's love and faithfulness, and I think everyone in attendance at creation knew where the story was going.

John Montgomery poetically proclaims this truth in his carol:

> *Angels from the realms of glory,*
> *Wing your flight o'er all the earth;*
> *Ye who sang creation's story*
> *Now proclaim Messiah's birth.*

The angels that sang over the spark of creation in Genesis also sang of Jesus's birth in Luke. And I believe those same angels will join the chorus in Revelation of "Holy, holy, holy is the Lord God Almighty, who was, and is, and is to come."

Consider these words about God from Isaiah 25:1: "In perfect faithfulness you have done wonderful things, things planned long ago" (NIV).

God is not making it up as He goes along. He's had Christmas Eve—an expectant day of hope for salvation—in mind since the very beginning. In God is Life, and that Life is the Light of all humankind.

The Light comes tomorrow. Prepare your heart. Prepare your soul. Prepare to come and worship, come and worship, worship Christ the newborn King!

The Gift of Christmas

It's here! Today is Christmas!

In the weeks leading up to this day, the presents have been slowly accumulating under the Christmas tree in my living room. Our girls—now ages five and two—are under no illusion that Santa brings all of the packages. The presents do not magically appear Christmas morning. One special gift does, yes, but the rest come from Mom and Dad.

The gifts are wrapped in fancy paper (with too much Scotch Tape) and topped with a sparkly bow. But what makes each present special is the label affixed to every package.

To Claire & Chloe
From Mom & Dad

When a person gives you a gift, they have specially selected it for you. They carefully deliver it to where they know you'll find it, and they address it so you know it's for you.

But the present isn't yours yet.

You can be holding a Christmas present in your hands, but until you have torn off the wrapping paper, opened the box, taken out the gift, and accepted it as your

·····>

····>

own, it is not yours. A gift can be given and never received.

And so it is with the gift of salvation. To be sure, salvation is a gift. Paul writes, "For the wages of sin is death, but the *gift of God* is eternal life in Christ Jesus our Lord" (Romans 6:23 NIV, my emphasis). But you have to accept it as your own.

Jesus came to this world to be a friend of sinners (Matthew 11:19, Luke 7:34). His mission was not to condemn the world, but to save it (John 3:17). And through Him and Him alone, we can receive salvation (Acts 4:12).

Have you accepted Jesus as your personal Lord and Savior? Have you accepted the gift of eternal life that He has written your name on? If not, what better day than Christmas to receive it?

It's as simple as this: say a prayer of confession that Jesus is Lord, and believe in your heart that God raised Him from the dead (Romans 10:9). Once you've made that declaration, you are a child of God! You are no longer chained to the mistakes, regrets, and fears of your past; you have received complete and unconditional redemption!

Ephesians 2:8 says, "God saved you by his grace when you believed. And you can't take credit for this; it is a gift from God" (NLT). What better gift could there be?

Today we celebrate the goodness of our God, the love of our Father, the presence of His Spirit, and the gift of Jesus.

From my family to yours:

Merry Christmas!

✦ Notes of Appreciation

This book was an absolute joy to write. Regardless as to whether anyone else ever reads it, it was a blessing to me, and I wish to thank the following individuals who had a hand in making this book possible.

To my beautiful wife, **Hanna**, for sharing my excitement and cheering me on. And for your patience as I pestered you to proofread the first draft. I love you to the moon and back!

To my Jesus-crooning friend (and beach buddy), ***Kathy Troccoli***, for the beautiful foreword you wrote for this book. I want to be you when I grow up!

To my senior pastor, ***Bob Beckler***, for your enthusiasm and support of this book. Your note meant more than you know.

To my ministry colleague and coffee connoisseur compadre, ***Cori Broddle***, for lending your discerning eyes and red pen to the final draft. You made this book erorr-free. (Next latte's on me.)

To my coach, ***Gina Wendt-Blasing***, for your encouragement. You're right: all it takes to start a book is 10 minutes of writing a day. Now it's your turn!

To these fine *photographers* from around the world who freely share their work on unsplash.com for others to use: Aaron Burden, Andre Benz, Annie Spratt, Aron Visuals, Clem Onojeghuo, Dan Kiefer, David Beale, Didi Miam, Evie Fjord, Hert Niks, Jake Goossen, Jeremy Bishop, Jeremy Gallman, Kelly Sikkema, Laura Nyhuis, Lore Schodts, Maria Vojtovicova, Matthias Kinsella, Nathan Fertig, Nick Fewings, Pawel Nolbert, Raspopova Marina, Richard Bell, Tobias Tullius, and Wil Stewart.

And finally, all praise, honor, and glory goes to **God** my Spiritual Dad, ***Jesus*** my Savior and friend, and the ***Holy Spirit*** my Helper—as it was in the beginning, is now, and ever shall be, world without end. Amen!

Soli Deo Gloria!

Made in the USA
Columbia, SC
14 November 2022

70931549R00072